Judy and Tom,

    So that you can recall your December, 2007 visit to Tulsa —

      Our best,

      Lacy & Al Whitehead

OKLAHOMA
simply beautiful

Photography by JIM ARGO, JOHN ELK III, *and* R. E. LINDSEY

FARCOUNTRY
PRESS

Right: The Antelope Hills. JOHN ELK III

Title page: Cedar Lake Park, Ouachita National Forest.
R. E. LINDSEY

Front cover: Wichita Mountains. JOHN ELK III

Back cover (top): Oklahoma proud. JIM ARGO

Back cover (bottom): Eastern Oklahoma. JOHN ELK III

ISBN 1-56037-228-1
Photographs © Jim Argo, John Elk III, and R. E. Lindsey/Lindsey Enterprises Inc.
© 2002 Farcountry Press

For more information on our books write: Farcountry Press,
P.O. Box 5630, Helena, MT 59604 or call: (800) 654-1105
or visit www.montanamagazine.com
Created, produced, and designed in the United States.
Printed in China

From the Photographers...

JOHN ELK III

I was born and went to school in Ponca City. Over the last ten years, I have been back on numerous occasions, visiting the cities, driving the back roads and stopping overnight in the many well-appointed state parks to enjoy the quiet and subtle beauty of the place.

Oklahoma is one of those places that reveals itself slowly, to those willing to take the time to look beyond the obvious. To really discover and appreciate the state you simply must get off the Interstates (of which Oklahoma has an amazing number), drive the smaller roads and be prepared to ask directions. From world-class museums to pioneer displays, from strenuous rock-climbing to quiet afternoons spent sitting in a fishing boat, there are enough different facets of Oklahoma to appeal to just about everyone.

I have my favorite places, some of which I'd love to share, others so special I'm almost tempted to keep them to myself. Certainly one of my favorites is the Wichita Mountains National Wildlife Preserve, with wonderful hiking through pink granite mountains and more wild animals to enjoy than anywhere in the U.S. outside Yellowstone. Getting to Black Mesa, far out in the Panhandle, takes hours of driving from almost anywhere, but the bluffs and badlands, dinosaur footprints and pioneer relics along the Santa Fe Trail make this another area well worth the effort to reach. Hundreds of miles to the East, the Talimena Scenic Drive, which runs along the spine of Winding Stair Mountain, offers mile after mile of stunning vistas out over the wooded countryside. I can't promise it will happen to you, but on two separate occasions while driving along this byway I had the thrill of seeing a black bear cross the road in front of me. In all of these more rural areas there are delightfully sited campgrounds in which to spend the night where, depending upon the season, you might hear bobwhites or whippoor-wills in the still, quiet mornings.

The two major cities of Oklahoma offer more obvious attractions. The newly refurbished and expanded National Cowboy and Western Heritage Museum in Oklahoma City is a world class facility, as is the Gilcrease Museum in Tulsa. Each time I visit the Oklahoma City National Memorial, which commemorates the terrorist bombing of the Murrah Federal Building, I have to take a few moments to deal with my emotions before I can begin my work. Visiting the Oklahoma City stockyards during auctions is a powerful taste of the Old West.

It's an amazing place, a state I'm very proud to call home.

JIM ARGO

I was born in Kansas but spent my childhood to young adulthood in Texas. While majoring in journalism at Texas Tech University, I was fortunate enough to spend some time assisting a *National Geographic* photographer. This everlasting visual impression propelled me into a career in photojournalism.

I moved to Oklahoma not knowing much about the state or its colorful history. My thoughts were of Rogers and Hammerstein's "Oklahoma!" with the wind sweeping down the plain and waving wheat that sure smelled sweet behind the rain.

For the next three decades my job as a photographer for the state's largest newspaper has allowed me to travel and photograph in all 77 counties. Large metropolitan centers such as Oklahoma City and Tulsa and the smallest communities, such as Kenton in the panhandle and Idabel in far southeast Oklahoma, have been subjects for my camera.

I have been to cattle roundups and even a buffalo roundup in the Tallgrass Prairie. I spent a year photographing German Mennonites and their life style and, on several occasions, two small Amish communities.

Farmers, ranchers, educators, chief executives, Native Americans and those who hold national and state public offices have all been in front of my camera lens. All are Oklahomans whose lives make up the everyday fabric of this great state.

Each year I spend four weeks or more traveling the state in search of different images. Often this means going back to locations I have photographed before. Maybe it's a different season; maybe the lighting is different, the early morning mist or the afterglow of a sunset; or maybe it's a place I just feel comfortable photographing.

Oklahoma's five geographic regions make it very difficult to create the one photograph that represents this state's image. I guess for me that is the exciting part.

R. E. LINDSEY

My father was a photographer with a kitchen darkroom before I was born. So I guess you could say I have photography in my blood. Little did I know when I picked up my first Kodak Pony camera at age six that photography would become a lifelong interest for me.

As an adult I realized that if I left the interstate highways to explore secondary roads, there is a lot of natural beauty to be found in Oklahoma. I started searching for wildflowers and my travels led me from the green hills of the Oklahoma Ozarks in the northeast to the ancient Quartz Mountains in the southwest. While criss-crossing the state for pleasure, I've discovered what a unique area Oklahoma is. Allow me to brag for a moment!

Oklahoma contains five very different geological areas, each with its own ecosystem. The northwestern part of the state contains high plains mesas covered with cactus and twenty-three rare plant species. The highest point in the state is the Black Mesa at the foothills of the Rocky Mountains. Dinosaur footprints can be found in a dry creek bed nearby. Autograph Rock, a short distance away, is where pioneers etched their names into the stone as they migrated west.

Just imagine traveling to the southeast part of the state to discover the Ouachita National Forest and fringed orchids. Lakes with islands are nestled in the deep hills, and cypress-lined rivers form oxbows. Spider lilies grow in the wetlands, and it is rumored that an occasional alligator can be found.

As I photograph Oklahoma, from the Oklahoma City National Memorial, historic cities or her native beauty, I am compelled to capture more of my native state on film. Through photography I have learned to appreciate the special place this is, and I have developed a genuine pride in a state I call home. Now if you'll excuse me, I feel a need to pack my camera and hit the road. Oklahoma's calling me again!

Above: On the Great Salt Plains. JOHN ELK III

Facing page: Sunset in Wichita Mountains Wildlife Refuge. JOHN ELK III

Right: Autumn mist rises from Beavers Bend Resort Park in southeastern Oklahoma. JIM ARGO

Below: Enjoying the Bar B Ranch near Beaver. JIM ARGO

Looking across Wichita Mountains Wildlife Refuge from Mount Scott. JOHN ELK III

Right: Each chair in the Oklahoma City National Memorial honors one of the 168 victims of the 1995 federal building bombing. JIM ARGO

Below: Gates of Time mark the moment of the April 19 explosion. JOHN ELK III

WE COME HERE TO REMEMBER
THOSE WHO WERE KILLED, THOSE WHO SURVIVED, AND THOSE CHANGED FOREVER.
MAY ALL WHO LEAVE HERE KNOW THE IMPACT OF VIOLENCE.
MAY THIS MEMORIAL OFFER COMFORT, STRENGTH, PEACE, HOPE AND SERENITY.

Above: Prairie sabatia near Collinsville. R. E. LINDSEY

Left: Foss State Park, west of Clinton, at sundown. R. E. LINDSEY

Right: Bricktown Historical District, once the site of warehouses, is Oklahoma City's newest entertainment district. JIM ARGO

Below: Oklahoma City skyline from Myriad Gardens. JOHN ELK III

Facing page: Mass ascension at Gatesway International Balloon Festival. R. E. LINDSEY

Left: The museum at Woolaroc Ranch, Bartlesville, houses an eclectic collection. JIM ARGO

Below: This State Capitol mural in Oklahoma City, by Chickasaw artist Mike Larsen, commemorates Oklahoma-born ballerinas Yvonne Chouteau, Rosella Hightower, Moscelyne Larkin, and Maria and Marjorie Tallchief. JIM ARGO

Facing page: Ponca City's 1927 movie palace. JOHN ELK III

Above: The Lodge at Woolaroc Ranch, Bartlesville. JOHN ELK III

Facing page: Glass Mountain in western Oklahoma. JOHN ELK III

Above: Leavenworth eryngo, despite its thistle-like appearance, is a member of the Carrot or Parsley family. R. E. LINDSEY

Right: Wildflowers color Quartz Mountain State Resort Park near Lone Wolf. R. E. LINDSEY

Above: Migrating pelicans visit the Salt Flats of north-central Oklahoma's Great Salt Plains State Park. JIM ARGO

Facing page: Enjoying Grand Lake near Grove. JIM ARGO

Above: Goat's rue grows in sandy prairie soil. R. E. LINDSEY

Left: Redbud trees, the Oklahoma state tree, in their delicate spring dress. JOHN ELK III

Facing page: In the Red Granite Mountains of Greer County. R. E. LINDSEY

Above: Barred owls range Oklahoma woodlands. R. E. LINDSEY

Left: The San Bois Mountains east of Wilburton. JOHN ELK III

Left: Purple windflower. R. E. LINDSEY

Below: Ready, set, and going at Turner Falls in the Arbuckle Mountains near Davis. JIM ARGO

Far left: Treasure Lake reflects a blue Oklahoma sky in Comanche County's Charon's Garden Wilderness Area. R. E. LINDSEY

Left: A collared lizard in the Cimarron River Valley. JOHN ELK III

Below: Petrified footprints are evidence that dinosaurs once roamed near Black Mesa. JOHN ELK III

The long view at Black Mesa. JOHN ELK III

Above: Autumn glory in McCurtain County. R. E. LINDSEY

Facing page: A climber tackles Mount Scott in the Wichitas. R. E. LINDSEY

Above: The National Drag Boat Races burn up Lake Overholser. JIM ARGO

Left: The Arkansas River flows through downtown Tulsa. R. E. LINDSEY

In the Panhandle. JOHN ELK III

Above: The Red Earth Festival at Oklahoma City. JIM ARGO

Right: Heavy-duty signage near Tonkawa. JOHN ELK III

Above: The restored Ferson Chapel at Watonga was dedicated on June 14, 1903. R. E. LINDSEY

Facing page: The peaceful Beaver Lodge Nature Trail in Beavers Bend Resort Park. R. E. LINDSEY

Left: In the Tall Grass Prairie Preserve in the Flint Hills.
JOHN ELK III

Below: Will Rogers Birthplace Ranch, Oologah. JOHN ELK III

Facing page: In the Wichita Mountains near Lawton.
JOHN ELK III

Winding Stair Mountain on the Talimena Scenic Byway, Le Flore County. R. E. LINDSEY

Exploring Devils Slide in Robbers Cave State Park, southeastern Oklahoma, which
gets its name for serving as a hideout for Jesse James and Belle Starr. R. E. LINDSEY

Right: The Illinois River making its way through Cherokee County. R. E. LINDSEY

Below: A surviving section of Route 66, near Vinita. JOHN ELK III

Dune buggies are welcome in Little Sahara State Park, south of Waynoka. JIM ARGO

Right: Blacktailed prairie dogs. JOHN ELK III

Below: Mount Scott sunset. JIM ARGO

Black Kettle National Grassland, near Cheyenne. JOHN ELK III

Above: Texas longhorns like this once trod the Chisholm Trail and other routes through Oklahoma Territory. JOHN ELK III

Right: Cedar Lake, Ouachita National Forest. JIM ARGO

Above: Roundup time in Cimarron County.

Facing page: The Cimarron River's flow near Freedom.

Right: Kaw Lake in north-central Oklahoma has one of the state's largest wintering bald eagle populations. R. E. LINDSEY

Below: Hominy, home to this mural, was named for Osage chief Ho Mo I ("Night Stalker"). JOHN ELK III

Foss State Park is a great place for waterskiing, paddleboating, swimming, horseback riding, camping, biking, and hiking. JOHN ELK III

Above and right: At Ponca City, visitors can tour the Marland Estate Mansion, home of E.W. Marland, one of Oklahoma's pioneer oilmen and its tenth governor. R. E. LINDSEY

Facing page: A quiet fall day along Beaver Creek, McCurtain County. R. E. LINDSEY

Above: Tallgrass Prairie Preserve. JIM ARGO

Facing page: Bison live in the Tallgrass Prairie Preserve
as they once did across most of the continent. JIM ARGO

Above: Alabaster Caverns State Park near Freedom allows visitors
to explore a large gypsum cave. JOHN ELK III

Facing page: The Festival of Lights decorates Shannon Springs Park
in Chickasha, southeast of Oklahoma City. R. E. LINDSEY

Above: In an Italian Renaissance villa, Tulsa's Philbrook Museum of Art exhibits an international collection. JOHN ELK III

Left: McGee Creek State Park near Farris offers horse and bicycle trails, hiking, primitive camping, and trail riding. R. E. LINDSEY

Above: Osage County redbuds and Cedar Creek. R. E. LINDSEY

Facing page: Oklahoma ranches may be feeding 360,000 head of cattle at any given time. JIM ARGO

Above: At the 101 Ranch Rodeo, Ponca City. JIM ARGO

Facing page: Panhandle thunderhead. JOHN ELK III

Lake Carlton in Robbers Cave State Park, near Wilburton. R. E. LINDSEY

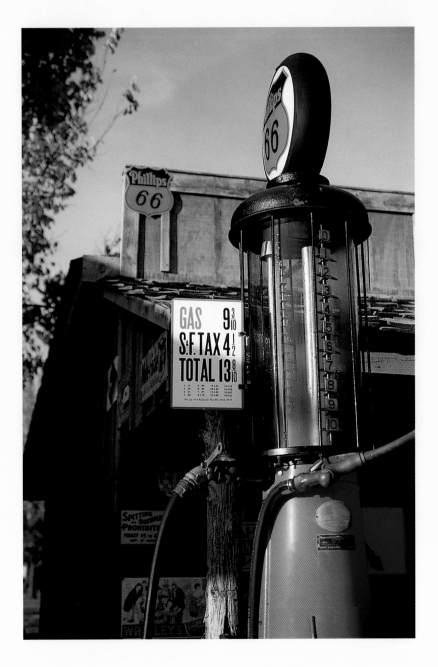

Above: A snail poses on one perfect leaf. R. E. LINDSEY

Left: In Sallisaw, the restored cabin of pioneer Judge Franklin Faulkner houses 14 Flags Museum, which includes this antique gasoline pump. R. E. LINDSEY

Right: At Kaw City. JIM ARGO

Below: Atchison, Topeka & Santa Fe
Railroad depot, Bartlesville. JIM ARGO

Bison in the Tallgrass Prairie Preserve. JOHN ELK III

Above: Exuberant sculpture in downtown Oklahoma City. R. E. LINDSEY

Facing page: Hulah Lake (from the Osage Indian word for "eagle") in northern Oklahoma's Wah-Sha-She State Park. JIM ARGO

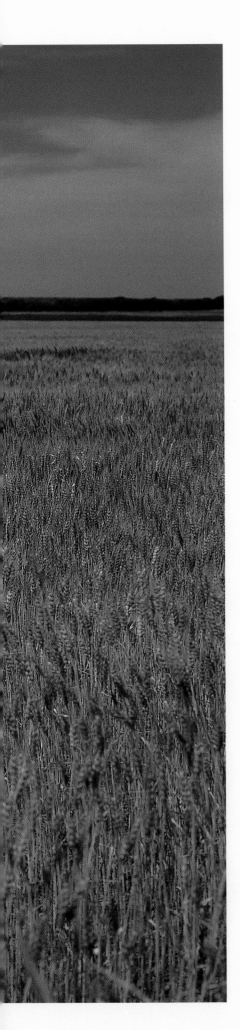

Left: Greer County wheat field. R. E. LINDSEY

Below: Wild turkeys' springtime mating display in Osage Hills State Park, in northeastern Oklahoma's wooded, rolling hills. R. E. LINDSEY

Human-powered boats are available for rental in Beavers Bend Resort Park (above),
for floating among the cypress trees (facing page). JOHN ELK III

Mexican hats bloom in eastern Oklahoma. JOHN ELK III

Sand Creek waterfalls, Osage Hills State Park. R. E. LINDSEY

Right: At Indian City USA—Anadarko's recreated Plains Indian village—this dancer prepares for war. JOHN ELK III

Left: The Antelope Hills in Roger Mills County rise above 2600 feet. JOHN ELK III

Below: The old mercantile at Kenton, in the Panhandle. JOHN ELK III

Above: A roadrunner blends in, Creek County. R. E. LINDSEY

Left: The open country of western Oklahoma. JOHN ELK III

Left: Sunset over Lake Carl Etling in the Panhandle. JOHN ELK III

Below: Prairie sunrise in the Wichitas. JOHN ELK III

Right: The former channel of Mountain Fork River holds an oxbow lake. R. E. LINDSEY

Below: Canada geese in Comanche County. R. E. LINDSEY

Morning breaks over Oologah Lake. JOHN ELK III

Above: Guthrie, Oklahoma's first state capital. JOHN ELK III

Right: Jackson County in Oklahoma's southwestern corner is the state's greatest cotton producer. JOHN ELK III

Above: Shattuck's Windmill Museum in Christmas garb. JIM ARGO

Right: McGee Creek Lake in a mauve mood. R. E. LINDSEY

Below: Lake Nanih Waiya in the southeast. <small>JOHN ELK III</small>

Right: Tallgrass prairie abloom. <small>R. E. LINDSEY</small>

At your service, on Lake Oologah. JOHN ELK III

Left: At a Tulsa Hispanic festival. R. E. LINDSEY

Below: Architectural detailing on the Tulsa Building in Tulsa. JIM ARGO

Above: Plains Indian tipis rise over Kaw Lake for a Boy Scout encampment.

Left: Elk Mountain.

Above: Carrizzo Creek below Black Mesa, Oklahoma's highest point at 4,973 feet. JIM ARGO

Facing page: Mount Scott. JIM ARGO

Above: Working Shawnee's rodeo. JIM ARGO

Left: Cimarron County wind power. JIM ARGO

99

Above: Sunrise on the prairie. JOHN ELK III

Facing page: Lake Murray in Lake Murray Resort Park near Ardmore. JIM ARGO

The ghost town of Lugert is under the waters of Lake Altus-Lugert,
Quartz Mountain Nature Park, in the southwest. JIM ARGO

Left: Raccoon on the alert. R. E. LINDSEY

Below: Mountain Fork River. JIM ARGO

"The Wedding Party" rock formation at Black Mesa. JIM ARGO

Right: White dogtooth violet. R. E. LINDSEY

Below: Autumn sunset on Sardis Lake. JIM ARGO

Above: Bull riding at the Oklahoma City Stockyard Fest. JIM ARGO

Facing page: Red granite giants on Elk Mountain. R. E. LINDSEY

Above: National Cowboy and Western Heritage Museum, Oklahoma City. JOHN ELK III

Right: Mountain Fork River is in southeastern Oklahoma's "Little Smokies" area. R. E. LINDSEY

Right: Tall thistle. R. E. LINDSEY

Below: Quanah Parker Lake, Wichita Wildlife
Refuge. JIM ARGO

Sunlight-and-cloud spectacle along Talimena Skyline Drive. JIM ARGO

Above: This central Oklahoma wheat field contributes to the state's nearly 4 million bushels of wheat a year. JOHN ELK III

Facing page: Trumpet vine with Lake Texoma in the background. JOHN ELK III

An eerie sunset on Highway 63 between Talihina and Big Cedar. JOHN ELK III

In northwestern Oklahoma's Glass Mountains. JIM ARGO

Above: Fly fishing the Mountain Fork River. JIM ARGO

Facing page: Indian blanket blossoms cover the Arbuckle Mountains. JOHN ELK III

Above: Fire from heaven on the open range. R. E. LINDSEY

Left: Along the David Boren Trail in Beavers Bend Resort Park near Broken Bow. JOHN ELK III

Black Mesa in the Panhandle. JOHN ELK III